C is for Cowboy

A Wyoming Alphabet

Written by Eugene Gagliano and Illustrated by Susan Guy

Sleeping Bear Press
310 North Main Street
Chelsea, MI 48118
www.sleepingbearpress.com

Sleeping Bear Press is an imprint of The Gale Group, Inc.,
a division of Thomson Learning, Inc.

Printed and bound in Canada.

10 9 8 7 6 5 4 3 2 1

Library of Congress Cataloging-in-Publication Data

Gagliano, Eugene M.
C is for cowboy : a Wyoming alphabet / by Eugene Gagliano ;
illustrated by Susan Guy.
p. cm.
Summary: An alphabet book that introduces Wyoming's history, culture,
and landscape, from the altitude of the Grand Tetons to an outdoorsman
named Jim Zumbo.
ISBN 1-58536-097-X
1. Wyoming—Juvenile literature. 2. English
language—Alphabet—Juvenile literature. [1. Wyoming. 2. Alphabet.] I.
Guy, Susan, 1948- ill. II. Title.
F761.3 .G34 2003
978.7—dc21   2003010470

Wyoming's People

Wyoming
A people's passion
Heartfelt aspirations
Praying, dreaming, seeking more.
People creasing the prairie carpet,
Crossing carousel streams of cottonwood.
People challenging the searing heat of summer
And the brittle cold of winter.
People taming the land with
Dust devil determination
And barbed wire.

Eugene M. Gagliano

A is for Altitude of mountains that soar;
    the Grand Tetons rise straight up from the floor.
    Called by many the Swiss Alps of our land,
        under star-scattered skies, these treasures stand.

The fault-block formation-mountains of the Tetons, running north and south on the western edge of Wyoming, dramatically rise 7,000 feet above the valley floor of Jackson Hole to a total height of 13,766 feet above sea level, and are considered by many to be the most majestic peaks in the continental United States. It is the most photographed mountain range in the world.

Twelve of the Teton peaks reach above 12,000 feet. The Tetons continue to grow at a rate of about one inch every 100 years.

Above 9,000 feet is the alpine tundra, where the growing season may be only two months long.

A a

B b

Robert Leroy Parker, alias Butch Cassidy, and Harry Longbaugh, alias the Sundance Kid, were notorious outlaws who robbed trains and stage-coaches. Cassidy's gang, the Wild Bunch, often escaped in the Bighorn Mountains to the Hole-in-the-Wall valley near Kaycee, Wyoming.

Butch Cassidy was known as the "gentleman outlaw" because he boasted never to have taken a life in any of his holdups.

Howard Eaton established Eaton's Guest Ranch, the first fully developed dude ranch in the Bighorn Mountains at the mouth of Wolf Canyon west of Sheridan, Wyoming. Today other well-known guest ranches include the HF Bar and Paradise near Buffalo, and Spear-O-Wigwam up the Red Grade Road near Big Horn, Wyoming.

The Bighorn Mountains begin with a B,
like the famous outlaw, Butch Cassidy,
who hid in a place called Hole-in-the-Wall,
listening to howls of the wild coyote's call.

SOUTHERN BIGHORN MOUNTAINS
THE HOLE
THE NOTCH
LAKE BED
N
HOLE IN THE WALL
Wyoming
$4,000 Reward
WILL BE PAID FOR THE CAPTURE OF
ROBERT LEROY PARKER
ALIAS
"BUTCH" CASSIDY

C
c

C is for Cattle, Cowgirl, and Cowboy;
at Cheyenne Frontier Days you will enjoy
the largest rodeo in all of the West—
watching rodeo's best of the best.

The annual 10-day Cheyenne Frontier Days celebration, which begins the last weekend in July, is known as the "Grand Daddy of Them All" and began as an annual "Old West Show" in 1897. People come from all over the United States and foreign countries to compete in bronc riding, calf roping, barrel racing, and bull riding events.

Chris LeDoux, former rodeo cowboy from Kaycee, Wyoming, won the world title in bareback riding in 1976. He was nominated for a Grammy for the hit single duet with Garth Brooks, "Whatcha Gonna Do with a Cowboy?" as best country vocal collaboration.

Many rodeo bronc and bull riding careers begin as young children ride sheep in rodeo events called mutton busting.

Devil's Tower is the core of an extinct volcano. This pillar of granite, which rises 1,280 feet, was declared to be the first national monument on September 24, 1906 by President Theodore Roosevelt.

The Kiowa Indians call it "Tso-aa," which means, "tree rock." Legend says that seven Indian girls being chased by a bear jumped on a low rock. As they prayed for help, the rock rose into the sky while the bear continued to claw at its base. The girls are still in the sky in the form of a group of seven small stars known as Pleiades.

The Arapaho, Cheyenne, Crow, and Sioux also have legends explaining the existence of Devil's Tower.

The movie *Close Encounters of the Third Kind* was filmed at Devil's Tower in 1977.

We know Devil's Tower starts with a D;
this giant rock you'll want to see.
The center of a volcano eroded away,
this national monument is here to stay.

Endangered species begins with **E**,
like the black-footed ferrets of Meeteetse.
Before they all died, and it was too late,
they were saved from extinction in our state.

The black-footed ferret was placed on the endangered species list in 1964. In August 1986 the last 15 known surviving black-footed ferrets were captured, when canine distemper was discovered in the only known wild ferret population. They were brought to a captive breeding facility, the Sybille Wildlife Research Unit near Wheatland, Wyoming. The program resulted in an increase of over 500 ferrets by 1991.

The successful reintroduction of juvenile ferrets began in 1991 in southeast Wyoming and in 1993 in Montana and South Dakota.

Not all protected animals remain on the endangered species list. Due to protective legislation, better land management, bans, and restricted use of pesticides the bald eagle, for example, has been removed from the list.

In 1924 Mrs. Nellie Tayloe Ross was elected governor after her husband, the former governor, died. Also, she was appointed the first woman director of the U.S. Mint in Washington, D.C., in April of 1933 and she lived to be 101 years old.

On December 10, 1869 the Equality State passed a law that gave women the right to vote. At the time no other state or territory gave women this right. The men who voted for this law thought it would encourage more women to move to Wyoming, which had a ratio of six men for each woman.

In 1870 Esther Hobart Morris became the first woman in the world to serve as justice of the peace, in South Pass City, Wyoming.

Wyoming has earned the name "Equality State" because of its historical support in the women's rights movement.

F stands for the First woman governor—
Ms. Nellie Tayloe Ross, and furthermore,
the Equality State has something to note.
Wyoming was first to let women vote.

It is estimated that approximately 100,000 grizzly bears once lived in the lower 48 states. Today only about 1% or 1,000 bears survive, and 90% of them can be found in Yellowstone Park.

The grizzly bear, found on the threatened species list, is the largest bear found in the continental United States. It is usually pale to dark brown in color with a prominent muscular hump over its shoulder. Guard hairs on the bear's fur may be silver or brown tipped giving them a "frosted" or "grizzled" look.

Male grizzly bears may weigh 400 to 650 pounds and reach seven to eight feet in length.

G g

G's for the Grizzly bear seen by roadside,
in Yellowstone Park, when taking a ride.
Wyoming has the largest grizzly population,
of all the contiguous states in the nation.

H stands for the Horse they called Steamboat.
The "horse that couldn't be ridden" we note.
All rodeo cowboys know this of course,
Steamboat's the most famous bucking horse.

Wild horses are the descendants of animals escaped from or released from Spanish explorers, ranchers, miners, U.S. Cavalry, or Native Americans.

Wyoming has several wild horse management areas where wild horses live in tightly knit bands made up of one stallion (male), a lead mare (female), and subordinate mares with their foals (babies less than a year old). A herd refers to all the bands that live in a certain area. In a band, the lead mare directs the band's movement in search of food and water, and keeps the other horses in line.

Steamboat was one of the best-known bucking horses of all time. He was known as the "horse that couldn't be ridden," and was thought to be the inspiration for the emblem on the Wyoming license plate.

I is for Indian paintbrush that grows
    along streams and hillsides, they make quite a show.
Perky state flower of orange, red, and rose,
    they spatter bright color across the meadows.

I i

The bright-colored "flowers" of the Indian paintbrush are actually colored bracts (leaves) like those of the poinsettia. These plants are parasitic and send down their root systems to feed off other plant roots, like its common host, the sagebrush. The color of paintbrush varies with the species, temperature, time of the year, altitude, and soil condition.

Upon the suggestion of Wyomingite Pat Henry, well-known author and illustrator, Tomie de Paola retold and illustrated *The Legend of the Indian Paintbrush* in 1988.

Jackalope begins with the letter J.
"Is there such a thing?" some people will say.
Rabbits with antlers may sound strange to you.
Come to Wyoming; this story is true.

In 1939, Douglas Herrick, a taxidermist, created the first "jackalope." After bagging a large jackrabbit, his hunting partners jokingly remarked how funny the animal would look with antlers on it.

The owner of the LaBonte Hotel in Douglas, Wyoming, bought the creation. One day a stranger entered the hotel and remarked, "Look, a jackalope." The name stuck. Since then, many imitations have been made and pictures of them appear on postcards.

J j

K k

The Bishop of Omaha, Nebraska selected Father William Kelly to preach to Catholics in Wyoming. There were no churches for the many Irish Catholic immigrants who came to help build the Union Pacific railroad in Wyoming. Father Kelly started the first Catholic Church in 1865 in Cheyenne. The church building was built in Omaha and shipped by railway to Cheyenne where it was set up. More churches were later built on land near the railroads donated by the Union Pacific.

K is for Father Kelly, summoned to teach.
Along the railroads he would preach.
While Irish workers did their labor,
he spread religion to his neighbor.

Along with the western meadowlark, horned larks and lark bunting are also found in Wyoming.

The western meadowlark creates a dome of grass on the ground for its nest, where it lays three to seven white or pink eggs speckled with brown or lavender. The male noisily protects its nest from intruders such as skunks, raccoons, weasels and hawks. Its diet consists of insects like caterpillars, grasshoppers, cutworms, and grain.

The song of the western meadowlark is flutelike and gurgling, and a distinctive sign of spring's arrival.

L l

L stands for Lark, Wyoming's state bird,
perched on a fencepost it can be heard.
Meadowlarks have a bright yellow breast
and sing the most beautiful song in the West.

m

M

M is for the famous Medicine Wheel.
Made out of rock and not out of steel,
by Native Americans we don't even know.
This mountaintop shrine was made long ago.

Located at the top of the Bighorn
Mountains, the medicine wheel is a
wheel-like formation made of rock that
has a circumference of about 250 feet.
It has a central cairn, or hub, that may
be symbolic of the sun and 28 spokes
that may represent the 28 lunar days.
Prehistoric Native Americans who
probably worshipped the sun built
this shrine.

According to Crow Indian legend, the
medicine wheel was used as a vision
quest site. A vision quest was the ritual
of a young male seeking to communcate
with the spirit world through visions.
These visions were brought on by fast-
ing, prayer, and other measures during
a time of isolation.

President Ulysses S. Grant signed a bill that made Yellowstone the first national park in the United States on March 1, 1872 "...as a pleasuring-ground for the benefit and enjoyment of the people."

In 1891 the United States Congress formed the first national forest, the Yellowstone Forest Reserve, which is now known as the Shoshone National Forest. Today, Wyoming has five national forests.

The federal government, because of its many national parks and monuments, owns one half of the land in Wyoming.

Tourism is Wyoming's second largest business after mining.

n
N

N is for National forest pleasures.
We were the first to have such treasures.
Great places to camp, hunt, fish, and bike,
to backpack, ride horses, picnic, and hike.

When surface water seeps down to meet the heat of the Earth's molten rock, hydrothermal activity occurs. In Yellowstone molten rock is only three miles below the surface, causing it to have the most varied and largest collection of hydrothermal features on Earth. Water passing over heated rock boils and turns to steam in some places under the park. The water and steam shoot up from time to time in high fountains called geysers. Yellowstone National Park boasts the world's most extensive area of geyser activity.

In geologic time, Old Faithful isn't that old. It has only been erupting for about 200 years. Old Faithful is the most well-known geyser because of its history of reliability. It erupts 18 to 21 times every day to an average height of 130 feet for 15 to 20 seconds, discharging about 5,000 to 8,000 gallons of water.

Steamboat geyser is the most powerful geyser in Yellowstone Park. It is irregular, but shoots water 300 to 350 feet into the air.

O for Old Faithful, all people should know,
the Yellowstone geyser makes such a show.
Tourists can watch it spout once every hour,
spraying its water-fountain-like shower.

Pp

P is for Pronghorn that prance on the plains.
You see them up-close from trucks, cars, and trains.
Our state has the largest herds in the West.
Come see the pronghorn, please be our guest.

The largest concentration of pronghorn antelope, found only in North America, is located in Wyoming. Herds of antelope can be seen grazing on the open plains and prairies, sagebrush flats, deserts, and foothills.

The pronghorn have long slender legs with firm, bouncy padded hooves that help make it the fastest running animal in North America. They have been clocked at 60 miles per hour, and their large eyes can see movement up to four miles away.

Pronghorn have true horns, which means they are hollow, unlike deer antlers that are solid.

Q stands for a Quivering cottonwood tree
named the largest one in the world to see.
This tree stood more than 60 feet tall,
which made this cottonwood biggest of all.

The plains cottonwood is the state tree. The largest cottonwood tree in America, with a circumference of 29 feet, used to be in Thermopolis before it died.

In 1990, as Wyoming was preparing to celebrate its statehood centennial, the Wyoming Chapter of the Society of American Foresters, a professional forestry organization, launched a contest to find a new state champion cottonwood. The winner was discovered on the Flying X Ranch. It stood 64 feet tall, measured 31 feet in circumference, and had an average crown spread just over 100 feet.

Cottonwoods aren't the oldest trees found in Wyoming though. Fossilized tree remains can be found at the Dry Creek Petrified Tree Area near Buffalo, Wyoming.

Qq

R is for Red Cloud, chief of the Oglala Sioux.
Joined by the Cheyenne and Arapaho too,
attacked a small fort called Platte Bridge Station,
to help save their land for the Indian nation.

The Sioux were one of the first tribes to wear eagle feathers in their hair or in a headdress to show the wearer's achievements. The famous war bonnet is derived from this.

Chief Red Cloud led the Native American resistance to the white invasion of the Powder River country from 1865-1868. He made peace with the whites in the Fort Laramie Treaty in November 1868, in exchange for the army's promise to abandon their Powder River forts.

Rr

The first sheep wagon was probably built about 1887 in Rawlins. Today, sheep wagons are prized by antique collectors. Owners proudly display them in parades and in their yards.

A lot of the sheepherders came from the Basque area of France and Spain. Basque sheepherders lived in sheep wagons year-round on the open range while tending their flocks of sheep. The wagons had a canvas cover or metal-covered top, and wooden or rubber wheels. They had all the basics such as a stove, table, bunk, and storage space.

A sleeping sheepherder might sometimes be awakened by a frightening racket and a violent shaking. A horse had decided to scratch itself on the corner of the sheep wagon. A loud shout and a thump would stop the intrusion.

The Basque people continue to keep their rich culture alive by sharing their songs and dances with the communities.

S is for sheep wagon, a mobile type home
　　where sheepherders live while their flocks roam.
You'll find them in backyards, on a mountainside,
　　in museums, on ranches, and prairies wide.

The first triceratops, a dinosaur 20 feet long with horns on its head, was discovered near Lance Creek in 1887. The paleontologist that discovered the skull thought it was a giant long-horned bison. Some scientists believe that triceratops roamed the land that is now Wyoming in herds near the end of the Cretaceous Period, some 65-68 million years ago.

The oldest fossils found in Wyoming are trilobites, early seashell-looking animals that lived in the sea.

The Como Bluffs Fossil Cabin was made from dinosaur bones found at Como Bluff. The cabin is around 80 years old, but "Ripley's Believe It or Not" called it the world's oldest building because of the dinosaur bone and mortar from which it was made.

Triceratops stands for the letter T.
The first one ever found for you and me.
This three-horned state dino used to roam
the land of Wyoming we now call home.

Wyoming leads the nation in coal production, averaging about 3 million tons per week. Centered in Campbell County, the Wyodak bed is the largest unbroken concentration of coal in the United States. An estimated 15 billion tons of useable coal is found there. The clean-burning, low-sulfur coal of Gillette, Wyoming is in high demand.

Most of Wyoming's mines are surface, or strip mines. When the mining is complete, land is reclaimed to a condition equal to or better than before the mining.

Wyoming coal is used primarily for electric power generation.

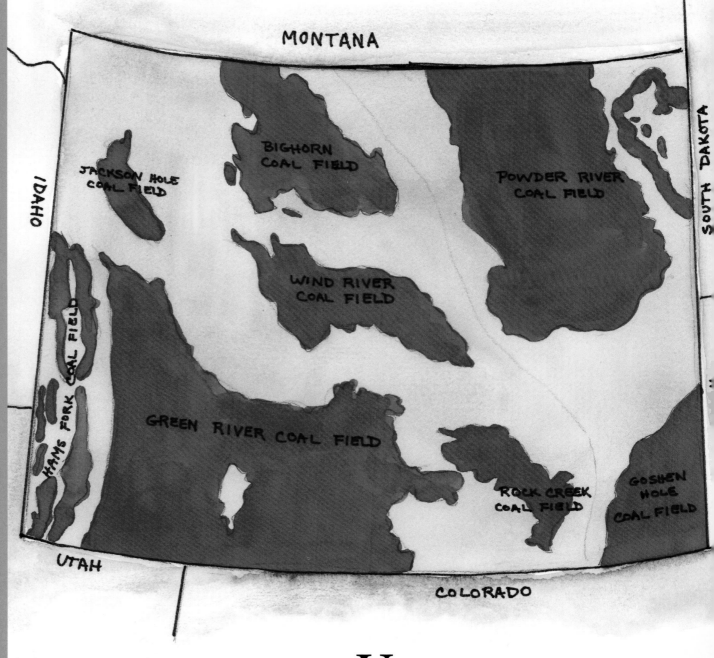

U is for Underground seams of coal
beneath the surface, just like a mole.
Our coal is the cleanest burning kind.
In our state it's not hard to find.

The Vore Buffalo Jump stands for V
an interesting historical site to see.
Come visit the town of Sundance too—
and see the mountain called Temple of the Sioux.

The Vore Buffalo Jump is located in the western fringe of the Wyoming Black Hills near Sundance, Wyoming. It is a gypsum sinkhole where prehistoric hunters skillfully maneuvered buffalo herds over a 50-foot cliff to their deaths. It is one of the largest sites of its kind on the Northwestern Plains.

The remains of about 20,000 buffalo have been revealed in the 22 levels of bone, reaching to a depth of 17 feet.

Throwing a weapon called an atlatl was another hunting method used to hunt buffalo before the introduction of the horse and bows and arrows.

The buffalo provided food, clothing, and shelter to the prehistoric hunters as well as to the Plains Indian tribes.

V
v

Wis for William F. Cody, or Buffalo Bill
whose Wild West Show gave many a thrill.
He was a showman, a Pony Express rider,
a western scout, rancher, and Indian fighter.

Colonel William Frederick Cody was perhaps one of the most famous Wyomingites. Nicknamed "Buffalo Bill," he supplied buffalo meat to workers on the Kansas Pacific Railroad during an 18-month period from 1867-1868. He reportedly killed 4,280 buffalo. The Native Americans called him "Pahaska" or "Yellow Hair."

Buffalo Bill owned the famous Sheridan Inn in Sheridan, Wyoming between the years of 1894-1896. It has been referred to as "The House of Sixty-Nine Gables." It was a social center where many famous guests stayed, such as Calamity Jane, presidents Theodore Roosevelt, Howard Taft, and Herbert Hoover, well-known author Ernest Hemingway, and famous western artist Charles Russell.

The Oregon Trail passes through the southern third of the state. Pioneers scratched their names into the rock known as Independence Rock, as a permanent testimony to their passage. Father De Smet called it the "Register of the Desert." You can still see the wagon wheel ruts at Oregon Trail Ruts State Historic Site south of Guernsey, Wyoming.

The Bozeman Trail was a faster, but a more dangerous route than the Overland Trail to the gold strike in Montana in 1862. It went through the center of the prime hunting grounds of the Sioux Indians. Fort Phil Kearny was built to protect the Bozeman Trail, which only lasted six travel seasons.

Fort Laramie was the place for many pioneers traveling the Oregon Trail on their way to claim land in Oregon, or heading for the gold fields in California during the gold rush of 1849.

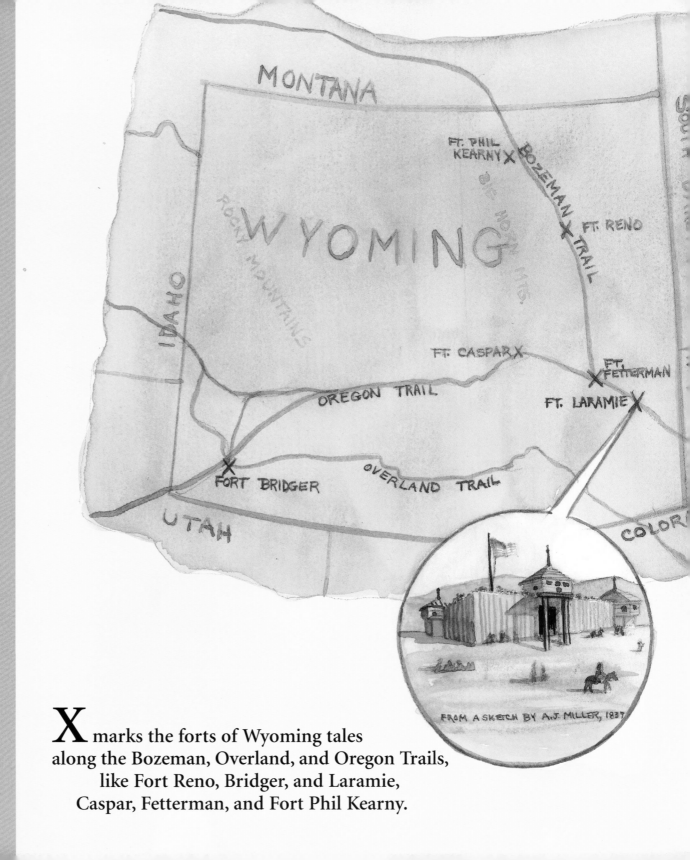

FROM A SKETCH BY A.J. MILLER, 1837

X marks the forts of Wyoming tales
along the Bozeman, Overland, and Oregon Trails,
like Fort Reno, Bridger, and Laramie,
Caspar, Fetterman, and Fort Phil Kearny.

Y y

Y stands for Yellowstone National Park
where you'll find yarrow and the meadowlark.
There're bison, grizzly, and geysers galore,
pelicans, eagles, waterfalls, and more.

Yellowstone National Park, created in 1872, was the world's first national park. Park visitors enjoy seeing the park's wildlife that includes black bear and grizzly bear, elk (wapiti), bison, moose, bighorn sheep, coyotes, lynx, mountain lions, trumpeter swans, bald eagles, and white pelican, to name just a few. Wolves have been reintroduced into the park and can also be seen.

The worst fires in the history of Yellowstone National Park occurred in 1988, when 995,000 acres burned, more than one-third of the park's area. Tourists can now see firsthand the rejuvenation, or regrowth of the forest in the park.

In Wyoming **Z** is for Zumbo, Jim by name,
hunting editor of *Outdoor Life* fame.
He writes, hunts, fishes, and cooks.
Enjoy any one of his videos or books.

Jim Zumbo has written over 1,000 articles for all the major outdoor magazines and has authored 21 books. An outdoor photographer, Jim has published 3,000 photographs. He has been a full-time editor for *Outdoor Life* magazine since 1978.

Widely regarded as the foremost authority on big game hunting in North America, Jim appears on such television networks as ESPN and TNN demonstrating a variety of hunting tips. He also hosts his own cooking show, the *Wild Gourmet*, on the Outdoor Channel. He has been cooking since college. After many years of traveling and hunting, and collecting wild game recipes, Jim has made a compilation of his favorite recipes.

A Geyser Full of Facts

1. What's called the "Grand Daddy of Them All"?
2. Who was the first woman governor of Wyoming?
3. Where did Butch Cassidy hide in the Bighorn Mountains?
4. What is taxidermist, Douglas Herrick, known for?
5. Name the state flower.
6. Near what town were the last black-footed ferrets found?
7. Where can you find the largest number of grizzly bears in Wyoming?
8. Which mountain range is often referred to as the "Swiss Alps of North America"?
9. Name the state bird and two things it eats.
10. The most famous geyser in Yellowstone National Park is _____ _____ .
11. Fort Phil Kearny was built to protect what famous trail?
12. Who is Kaycee, Wyoming's well-known country music artist?
13. Devil's Tower is the center of an extinct _____.
14. Steamboat was a famous bull. True or False
15. What is the name of an important Native American mountaintop shrine?
16. When was Yellowstone National Park created?
17. What's another name for William F. Cody?
18. The _____ _____ is only found in North America.
19. What is Wyoming's nickname?
20. Who started the first Catholic Church in Cheyenne?

1. Cheyenne Frontier Days
2. Nellie Tayloe Ross
3. Hole-in-the-Wall
4. The Jackalope
5. Indian Paintbrush
6. Meeteetse, Wyoming
7. Yellowstone National Park
8. The Tetons
9. Western meadowlark. It eats caterpillars, grasshoppers, cutworms, and grains.
10. Old Faithful
11. The Bozeman Trail
12. Chris LeDoux
13. Volcano
14. False. Steamboat was a famous bucking bronc.
15. The Medicine Wheel
16. In 1872
17. Buffalo Bill
18. Pronghorn antelope
19. The Equality State
20. Father William Kelly

Eugene Gagliano

Known by many children as the "teacher who dances on his desk," Gene Gagliano is an elementary schoolteacher and writer with a great sense of humor, who lives with his wife Carol at the base of the Bighorn Mountains in Buffalo, Wyoming. He loves children and has four of his own, Gina, Jared, Darin, Nathan and son-in-law, Ron. A member of the Wyoming Writers, and the Society of Children's Book Writers and Illustrators, Gene has been published in *Chicken Soup for the Preteen Soul*, and his first book entitled *Secret of the Black Widow*, was published in 2002. Gene and Carol are members of a professional singing group, the Polyester Blends. He enjoys making his educational and entertaining school visits, as well as hiking, canoeing, gardening, and painting.

Susan Guy

Award winning artist Susan Guy is known for her colorful paintings of equine and western themes. Her work is displayed in numerous galleries and exhibitions across the country, such as the prestigious Arts for the Parks competition in Jackson, Wyoming, and the American Academy of Equine Art in Lexington, Kentucky. One of her paintings is also included in the permanent collection of the Phippen Museum in Prescott, Arizona. She is a signature member of the American Academy of Women Artists.